Brus

Johan Reygaerts

Photographs
Hugo Maertens

lannoo

In 1979 the city of Brussels celebrated its millennium. More than a thousand years of history have unfolded since the days of the fortified camp on the banks of the Zenne, a thousand years during which it mushroomed into the nineteen municipalities which together comprise the Brussels Region, since 1989 one of the Regions of the federal kingdom of Belgium, with its own Regional government and directly elected parliament.

For a large proportion of their history, the people of Brussels have had to live under foreign rulers, from the kindly Archduke Albrecht and Archduchess Isabella to dreaded tyrants like the Duke of Alva. Today it is the Europeans who have descended on Brussels —fortunately with better intentions than the many invaders and rulers who have terrorised the town through the ages. Brussels cherishes an ambition to become the capital of Europe, or more precisely, the European Community, and it is going all out to achieve this aim. Some of the concessions which this entails are rather extreme, but this does not appear to worry the people of Brussels unduly. They see a great international future for Brussels, playing for Europe the role of Washington DC in the United States.

On the Grote Markt (main square) 'seven' is the magic number. It was from here that seven patrician dynasties once ruled over the seven districts of Brussels, spread over seven hills - known here as 'mountains'.

This has all meant that Brussels has become busier and busier over the last few years. Housing the headquarters of both NATO and the EC implies the influx of a host of delegations living and working in the city. Some countries have more than one ambassador in Brussels. And Brussels also has one of the highest concentrations of press representatives in the world.

The city is alive with journalists: there are far more press men than restaurants or cafés in Brussels —and that is saying something !

Alongside all this, the people of Brussels live their lives at their own pace, in this two-speed city. There is the fast-lane official life of the kingdom, with its rulers and representatives, international bodies like NATO and the EG, the Flemish government, the Belgian government and the parliaments. Next door to all this, the people of Brussels themselves live and work scattered over dozens of villages and parishes, each huddled around its own church spire. In many of these parishes, you will still find a cosy village atmosphere, right down to the lively village fair. But village life is gradually fading away in the parishes of Brussels. These villages are parcelled together in no less than nineteen different municipalities, each with its own administrators, municipal council and passionately defended policies. And every municipality has its own Mayor at the helm.

There is a growing feeling that these little 'Principalities' and their 'Prince-Bishops' should be relegated to the history books, because they make it so difficult for a general policy to be put into practice for the huge Brussels

agglomeration as a whole, let alone the Brussels Region.

This all sounds very serious, but the rest of this book will make it quite clear that life in Brussels is far from stiff and straight-laced. Brussels is above all a Burgundian city where life is lived to the full, and its people still share the joyous appetite for living that radiates from Breughel's paintings.

Brussels, a city to love.

Open-air cafés on the Grote Markt (main square), which dates largely from after 1695, when the centre of Brussels was reduced to ruins on the orders of the French Sun King.

Foreign rulers, like Charles of Lorraine, sometimes proved to be a blessing in disguise for Brussels.
This eighteenth-century Austrian governor was in command of the German Order.

The counts of Egmond and Horne, seen here standing serenely side by side on their pedestal on the Kleine Zavel (Petit Sablon), were beheaded by Alva, the tyrannical Spanish ruler who created a massacre in Brussels, too.

There is the official Brussels, like the Palace of the Nation, the national parliament, seen here.

above
Many travellers arrive in Brussels at Central Station, built by the famous art nouveau architect, Victor Horta.

left
Since independence in 1830, foreign invaders have had to contend with Belgium's own men.

above
Brussels' business world is
flourishing as well. The whole
world wants an office near the
EC.

right
The concentration of offices is
becoming greater by the day to the
extent that they are gradually
taking over the capital.
The world press, company
headquarters, banks, embassies and
other representative bodies all
congregate here.

St. Jacob-op-de-Coudenberg (St. James-on-Couden-Mountain) is the cathedral of the bishopric of the armed forces and also the parish church of Brussels' most thinly-populated community:
only fifty-two parishioners, including King Boudewijn, live beneath the tower of this church.
The legendary crusader, Godfried van Bouillon, holds the banner high in up-town Brussels.

The Zoniënwoud (forest) is an oasis of peace in the capital.

left
A small palace in
Regentschapsstraat (Regency
Street), where King Albert I was
born and which is now home to the
Audit Office.

above
A little house with a balcony garden
at the front. Brussels has something
for everyone !

Brussels seven times seven

In Brussels 'sevens' are trumps ! And there are at least seven examples of things sevenfold in Brussels, as many sharp observers and connoisseurs of the city have discovered. Puteanus even wrote a poem celebrating the magical seven-ness of Brussels: 'Bruxella Septenaria'.

For a start, 'Brussel', the Dutch name for Brussels, which was originally a Flemish town, has *seven letters*.

And in common with quite a number of other international cities, Brussels was built over the centuries on *seven hills* ! But to the inhabitants of our metropolis, 'hills' are not good enough —so, with a touch of vanity (and perhaps seven grams of pride ?) they prefer to call them 'mountains'. These seven impressive peaks are the Coudenberg, Galgenberg, Kunstberg, Molenberg, Reuzenberg, Treurenberg and Warmoesberg. Brussels also has *seven quarters* or districts, formerly *seven parishes*. The most famous of these is the Grote Markt or main market square, 'the most beautiful square in the world' and an absolute must for even the busiest tourist passing through on a high-speed trip. In addition to this, there are six other quarters which the burghers of Brussels still know by name today —but only just: the Boerenwijk (Farmers' quarter), Havenwijk (Dock quarter), Marollen, Paleizenwijk (Palaces quarter), Zavel (Sand quarter) and Sint-Goriks, which was the cradle of Brussels.

Seven families called the tune in Brussels in the Middle Ages. Five of these families had names which started with 'S': Serhuygs, Seroeloffs, Sleeus, Steenweeghe and Sweerts. Coudenbergh and Rodenbeecke are exceptions, but no less powerful for that !

Seven streets lead into the Market Square, as the apotheosis of the magical sevens.

And finally, just as in ancient Thebe, there are the *seven city gates* of both the first and the second city walls.

The remarkably intact and elegant façades of the Grote Markt (main square) still reflect the power and wealth of the guilds.

above
The Halle Gate was one of the
seven gateways in the city's second
ramparts which were built in the
fourteenth century. Like Thebes,
Brussels had seven city gates.

right
A walk through the streets of
Brussels quickly reveals the city's
amazingly rich cultural past.

left
Seven streets debouch into the
Grote Markt (main square).
The Boterstraat, the oldest,
time-honoured trade route,
is one of them.

Atomium, lace and Manneken Pis

All over the world, nine balls and a chubby little boy are the symbols of Brussels, and even of Belgium as a whole. Hasty tourists from every corner of the earth feel they *must* see at least two sights in every capital, come what may, and pose cheesily in front of them for the traditional snaps. Manneken Pis and Atomium are for Brussels and the nation what windmills and tulips are for the Netherlands, and the Eiffel Tower for Paris and France.

In addition to these two symbols, lace also occupies an important place. The many lace shops on and around the Grote Markt clearly show that Brussels lace —other sorts are sold as well— is another of the capital's labels.

Lace makers from the working classes, often children, used to work for low wages, while the delicate pieces of textile they produced were usually sold at exorbitant prices. A piece of Brussels lace was a present fit even for a queen, as the many pieces in the royal collection illustrate.

In Brussels, numerous technical improvements were introduced into lace production, such as lace designs on a woven background.

Today the so-called old Brussels lace which is sold in the capital's lace shops, is made by hand in the Far East. Those who want to see the real thing will be able to look at a few museum pieces in some of the shops, but would do best to go along to the Museum of Costumes and Lace in the Violetstraat behind the Town Hall. Contemporary production is fostered at a lace atelier and school on the top floor. The Queen lends her gracious patronage to this ancient art.

left
Lace is one of Brussels' visiting cards. However, the industrious lace makers of the olden days were not surrounded by as much gold as the worker on this signboard.

THE OLDEST INHABITANT OF THE TOWN

Manneken Pis is on the corner of the Stoofstraat. The name of the street —Stove Street— refers to the large boiler which was used to produce steam for the Turkish baths available there. In previous ages, Turkish baths in Brussels also operated as brothels, so it is natural enough to find the little chap watering the street so shamelessly here.

There are any number of tales and legends claiming to explain the origins of this little statue, but no one knows what the true story is. One version tells of a rich burgher who commissioned the statue and its fountain to commemorate his joy at finding his little son after losing him during a celebration in the streets of Brussels. The little boy was found on this very corner, relieving himself without a trace of modesty, where now a bronze Manneken Pis continues to do the same for posterity. Another, more heroic tale is that in the thirteenth century, a little boy put out the fuse of a devilish enemy weapon with 'the only water that he could lay his hands on', thus saving Brussels from a great disaster. An action statue was made to commemorate this heroic deed, and erected on a pedestal at the scene of the event.

But this explanation is more amusing. A knight's son, who was already in love despite his tender age —and with no one less than Saint Goedele, the celebrated patroness of Brussels— once stopped at the corner of the Stoofstraat to urinate against a hermit's front door. Naturally, the hermit was none too pleased, and turned the knight's son into stone, condemning him to stand there as a fountain for ever. But it is odd that the hermit who reacted so furiously to the little boy's bodily functions, had chosen to live in a red light district!

But whatever his history may be, Manneken Pis as we know him today is a bronze statue made by the famous baroque sculptor Jérôme Duquesnoy, commissioned by the Brussels City Council in 1619. However, this is not the oldest version of Manneken Pis. In Geraardsbergen in East Flanders, a similar fountain has been in action for 160 years longer —since 1459.

A text dating from 1377 refers to a statue of the same kind which decorated a fountain on the corner of the Stoofstraat. This statue was of stone, while the bronze version dates from 250 years later.

Manneken Pis in Brussels has an impressive wardrobe of hundreds of costumes, and a special selection of his outfits can be admired in the *Manneken Pis Museum* in the Broodhuis on the Market Square. The oldest costume was a gift from Maximilian of Bavaria, and dates from 1698. The shameless little chap has his staff to attend to his every need: an official dresser to help him in and out of his clothes —quite tricky, given his normal stance— and two maids. But after all, *noblesse oblige*, and that certainly applies to the oldest inhabitant of the city.

The gossamer-fine Brussels lace is very delicate.
Kilometres of lace travel to the furthest corners of the globe in suitcases and travel bags.

Manneken Pis,
the 'city's oldest citizen'.

AN IRON CRYSTAL 160 BILLION TIMES LARGER THAN LIFE

Another remarkable sight is *Atomium*, a highly unusual monument over 100 metres high created as the symbol of the World Exhibition of 1958, and belief in progress and the future. And it was almost consigned to the rubbish tip not so very long ago ! But there it still stands: an iron crystal 160 billion times enlarged, with nine spherical atoms each weighing 200 tonnes linked by tubular shafts enclosing stairs and escalators. As a progressive finishing touch, Atomium's designing engineer A. Waterkeyn came up with the fastest lift in the world for his monument.

above
In the immediate vicinity of the Atomium, Copernicus keeps a strict eye on the universe.

left
The Atomium, symbol of the 1958 World Fair, is in fact an iron crystal consisting of nine atoms enlarged 160 billion times.

Brussels: many sing her praises

IN MYSTERIOUS HARMONY

Brussels is flourishing, prosperous, charming. But the secret of this success remains a mystery. Brussels is like a 'choir for poor singers': plenty of voices are off-key, but most of the singers are doing their best, and together they blend into a miraculously pleasing if not perfect harmony. But then the people of Brussels are not choirboys!

Under the influence of too much Geuze beer, men are apt to wax lyrical and praise Brussels as a veiled beauty whose heady delights emerge more and more clearly as the veils are gently removed. But the observer who stays too sober may see no more than a faded courtesan who has lost her charms. People are never unanimous about Brussels. Northerners see the traffic in Brussels as a madhouse, while Southerners miss the hooting-tooting third-world clamour of their own city streets.

A certain highly-placed Brussels magistrate has a clock on his wall which does everything in reverse. Even the hands of the clock turn anti-clockwise, while the clock face bears an inscription that 'Nothing is logical in Belgium'.

This is even more true of Brussels! The wheels may be square, but they do keep turning, and that's the most important thing for most of us here in the capital city. If everything ran smoothly and predictably, it would leave little scope for the odd deviation from the straight and narrow, the innocent peccadilloes that are the spice of life. And of all the Belgians, the people of Brussels relish a bite of forbidden fruit the most.

What makes Brussels so special is that it is one of the charmed circle of international capital cities whose special charm and energy derive from sharp contrasts.

Why was Berlin so fascinating? Because it was the home ground of two battling ideologies: capitalism and communism.

What makes Istanbul so special? The dividing line between two great religions, Christianity and Islam, which runs through the heart of the city.

And how does Brussels qualify for membership of this remarkable group? By being the main interface between two great cultures, the Latin and the Germanic, in constant conflict here, flaring up one day and dying down again the next.

Although the size and number of inhabitants of Brussels are not comparable with other great capital cities of the world, it is indisputably a cosmopolitan metropolis, if on a smaller scale. With the EC headquarters located in Brussels, world leaders regularly stop off here, lending the city some of the international glamour of a Washington DC, as our capital grows in stature. Brussels has already acquired the status of independent metropolitan Region, one of the three Regions of Belgium. Perhaps in years to come it may even become 'Brussels DB' —'District of Belgium'!

left
The St. Hubert Gallery, Europe's first covered shopping street, was built in 1846.

above
The on-going tussle between two cultures, which occasionally really let fly at each other in Brussels, make the Belgian capital city a most unusual place, where tension is never far from the surface.

right
Wetstraat 16 (Law Street), the Prime Minister's residence, is a much-visited address. World leaders and heads of state come and go during their visits to the EC and NATO in Brussels, thereby underlining the growing importance of the capital.

The people of Brussels have never really been sure if they should be proud of their inland sea port.

ROME ON THE ZENNE

Compare Brussels with other great cities of the world, and you will find it comes out with flying colours. 'Rome on the Zenne' would be a fitting title, for although the Zenne is not a mighty river but an underground trickle, the mentality of the inhabitants of the Eternal City is very similar to that of the people of Brussels. The temperament of the Romans is perhaps more fiery, but our metropolitans are also famous for their sudden outbursts of 'Spanish fury' ! Life in this proud city of Brabant has a distinctly Italian flavour. The proof ? Italians living in Brussels are rarely homesick ! They feel quite at home here from the very first day, skilfully negotiating their way around all manner of problems and obstacles, just like the locals.

Both Brussels and Rome are the capital cities of nations created and launched with operatic verve in the nineteenth century. In Italy, unification was linked with operas by Verdi, and in Brussels revolution broke out after a badly-sung opera —'De Stomme van Portici'— in the Muntschouwburg.

Operetta performances are also very popular —particularly on the high-comedy political scene, where governments fall on the proverbial banana skins, to everyone's delight. And there is no shortage of banana skins !

Congress Column, with the statue of the first Belgian king, Leopold I,
is an unwavering symbol of the Belgian state. Below it burns the eternal flame.

While such dramas are played out against the quickly-changing background of the city, the people of Brussels certainly do not behave like wooden puppets, despite their enthusiasm for the art of marionette theatre, one of the highlights of the arts world here. Just as their kindred spirits in Rome, the people of Brussels do their best to set an example for the rest of their countrymen in swindling the State. Belgians regard the national authorities as a foreign object in the body politic —something they distrust and feel no solidarity with.

This is perhaps hardly surprising, since few European towns have groaned under as many foreign oppressors and conquerors as Brussels. It is natural enough that her people should have developed a legendary repertoire of 'con tricks' in the course of the long ages of oppression, so that they could lead the central and municipal authorities up the garden path, if necessary. The people of Brussels, who consider themselves to be the only true and genuine Belgians, pride themselves on their dazzling shrewdness in evading the laws of the land. They never fail to seize an opportunity to rip off the bureaucrats —and then carry on with their business in all serenity until the next opportunity arises.

Independent spirits, you might call them, or perhaps simply

pig-headed. They will let events take their course patiently enough in the beginning, but at the end of the day, what they don't want or don't like has no hope of getting off the ground. Centuries ago, the people of Brussels decided that they did not want a university in Brussels. Why? Because they wanted to protect the virginity of their daughters at all costs —you never know what might happen in a town overrun with students on the binge. So the university could go and knock on someone else's door. It did just that, and became the

prestigious Catholic University of Louvain.

The statue topping the once so fashionable Hotel Métropole on the Brouckère Square is a perfect —if unintentional— personification of the spirit of Brussels. The sculptured lady perched on the lofty tympanum looks rather like a smaller version of the Statue of Liberty in New York. She symbolises 'Progress', wearing a crown of light and bearing a torch to enlighten the world. A luminous idea... but such a pity that they had to use economy lamps...

This lady at the foot of the triumphal arch in Jubelpark (Jubilee Park) has been keeping an eye on things since the kingdom's fiftieth anniversary.

The Pavilion of Leopold I in Laken Park;
a small neo-Gothic temple with a fine spire.

above
Mellaerts ponds in Woluwe Park
where you can go canoeing and
fish.

below
Factory chimneys in Vilvoorde.

right
This stone elephant stands in
the square in front of the
Royal Museum of Central Africa
in Tervuren.

Lazing in the sun in Woluwe Park. It is thanks to Leopold II that this little piece of nature has been preserved.

The citizens of the metropolis are
fond of peace and quiet and so still
manage to find a tranquil spot
for a rest.

above
Desiderius Erasmus stayed in this grand house in 1521 and was homesick for Anderlecht for the rest of his life. The house is now the 'Home of Erasmus', a museum containing manuscripts by the great humanist and engravings by Holbein.

below
The Beguinage in Anderlecht, the home of God-fearing women, beguines of modest origins, as the architecture and scale suggest.

right
The Grote Markt (main square) is at its most beautiful on weekdays when the flower stalls are out under their red and green parasols, the colours of the city.

Brussels has become Babel with voices from everywhere, even at the daily flea market.

Zooming in on the melting pot of Brussels

Like any other town with a cosmopolitan character and aspirations, Brussels has become a melting pot of peoples and cultures. The sometimes violent confrontation of the two great cultures in Brussels, the Latin and Germanic, is nothing new. But the growing influx of the most diverse peoples, cultures and religions has brought a refreshing wind of change to the capital, stimulating and enriching the quality of life. With its aging population, an injection of young blood was just what Brussels needed to stop it slipping into senility ! When the European institutions were set up in Brussels, with its ambition to be the capital of the West, it became even more of an international honeypot. As the seat of the EC, Brussels acts like a magnet for almost all the peoples and cultures of the world. Life is good in Europe, and certainly in the capital, relatively speaking, and a host of people want to get as close as possible to the fleshpots of Europe.

Until quite recently, the presence of the European Commission, European Parliament and European administration posed no real problems in Brussels. But then the cost of living in Brussels shot up over a short period of time, and the price of its international ambitions now has to be paid. The people of Europe are no longer creeping in and taking us by surprise: they are charging in on all sides !

And now Brussels is in danger of becoming a town where all its citizens have equal rights and duties, but some are more equal than others, and the less fortunate groups end up in dismal ghettos. The example of Washington is a dire warning of what could happen here !

The Europeans and other peoples who have settled in Brussels naturally brought their own recipes and culinary secrets with them. These have found their way into the restaurants and bistros of Brussels, adding yet more variety to the already bewildering choice of dishes on their lengthy menus. The gentle art of eating well takes precedence in Brussels !

Dozens of different religions are practised in Brussels: Roman Catholic services are held in almost forty different languages, for a start. And it broadens one's horizons to realise that more than 110 different nationalities live side by side in a municipality like Sint-Gillis, to name just one example. The spicy aroma of its exotic markets and the colourful, unfamiliar street scenes —sometimes far from up-tight and tidy— are now characteristic features of Sint Gillis.

And much regretted by those who do not see this ethnic enrichment in a positive light.

The European Community in Brussels stands for a rich multiplicity of cultures, languages, religions and political persuasions.

above
And on the Grote Markt (main square), too, everyone is welcome. Faces and colours from all over the world enjoy its beauty.

left
Exotic songs rejuvenate the local population and bring colour and sound to metropolitan life.

above
Other continents and cultures are never far from the Brussels antique shops and the art trade either. So the head of a meter-high percussion instrument from Polynesia dominates the vista through a Brussels alleyway near the Zavel (Sablon).

left
The black population of Africa brought the country and its capital much wealth and prosperity during the Belgian colonisation of the Congo, as sculptures in various parts of the city reflect. And in the Matonge district of Elsene (Ixelles) animated goings-on are part and parcel of everyday life, because this is the home of many Zaireans with their perpetual laugh and inborn good humour.

King Leopold II had the imposing Royal Museum of Central Africa built in Tervuren Park,
where the culture and history of Central Africa can be admired.

right
The Roman Catholic rites alone are celebrated in more than forty languages in this city; for example, in the splendid late-Gothic Church of the Sablon.

right
Every day the prayers and songs of scores of religions rise to the many gods above the Brussels atmosphere. This little tower surmounts the Russian orthodox church of the tsarists in Ukkel.

left
An increasing number of Eastern Europeans are settling in the capital, where they perform classical music in the streets and alleyways.

Following pages
Even on the Flea Market the whole world is represented. Native Santa Clauses and saints from numerous other countries stand alongside sturdy Japanese warriors, sizeable Chinese vases, delicate Indonesian bird cages and looking glasses with no glass. They do have one thing in common, however: they are all for sale!

The belly of Brussels

ALWAYS READY FOR MORE

The people of Brussels enjoy the nickname of 'kiekenfretters' or chicken chewers, although what they find on their plate is usually a cockerel. And moreover, the insatiable appetite of the Burgundian eaters in our capital is not confined to chicken, or even the dainty pullets you can polish off at 'Comme chez Soi' with its three stars —that is, if you reserve your table in advance, of course, and do not forget to wear a tie...

Paris, Lyon and Brussels together form the reigning triumvirate of cities with the best food in the world. And it must be admitted that the culinary delights of Brussels are far superior to those of the 'City of Light', which does not even have its own individual cuisine, unlike our capital city. In all corners of the world, discerning eaters know that cooks in and around Brussels have kept faith with the traditional Burgundian cuisine, preserving it and improving on it with love and devotion. They had no need to gild their art with short-lived novelties or fashionable gimmicks. Enough said ! If the Parisians themselves pop over to Brussels now and then for a good meal, the conclusion is clear. In fact, the chefs of Brussels are not always interested in winning their French stars: one of them went so far as to hang up a notice on his door refusing all entrance to inspectors anxious to award stars —even the right sort of inspector !

But now let us take a tour of the typical dishes of Brussels.

MUSSELS ?
THIS MUST BE BRUSSELS !

Sprouts, known all over the world as 'Brussels sprouts', were once picked as tiny cabbages on the hillside of Sint-Gillis, which is now one of the nineteen municipalities of Brussels. They are delicious and quite irresistible served with potatoes and a pork chop from a free-range Brabant pig with a good life in the open air behind him !

Another jewel in the crown of the Brussels cuisine is 'stoemp' or 'mash'. If they served that in heaven, the saints would turn up their noses at ambrosia, with or without a golden spoon ! 'Stoemp' is very simple to prepare. Boil some potatoes, which by the way are not regarded as a vegetable in Brussels —or indeed anywhere in Belgium— but are considered to be in a class of their own. At the same time, boil a vegetable, preferably cabbage or spinach. Now drain the potatoes and the vegetable and mash them up together to make a colourful purée. If you eat it in a restaurant, show the waiter that you are a connoisseur by making a well in the middle and asking him to fill it with the fatty juices from the meat, which are usually very tasty. Mix it all up together, and it is food for the gods ! Garnish it with crunchy snippets of fried bacon, and eat it with a couple of thick slices of streaky bacon, black pudding (or white), or sausages.

A Catholic ex-Prime Minister who was Minister of State at the time, was once given a grilling for allegedly trying to curry favour with the people of Brussels at election time by handing out a free meal of black pudding. That was

A morsel from the belly of Brussels with its insatiable stomach.
In the middle: 'Chez Leon',
the king of mussels with chips.
'Mussels ? This must be Brussels !'

above
'Chez Jean' serves good
home-cooking Burgundian-style.
This is one of the many traditional
establishments; so Brussels that
even the Mayor is a 'habitué' here.

right
Every day glaciers of ice are moved
into the 'Ilot Sacré' (Sacred Little
Island) and mountains of food are
displayed on top of them.
It is important to cater to the eye as
well !

against the election rules, and really made the feathers fly in the political world. But the politician in question couldn't see the problem at all, and shrugged it off with a laconic 'all that fuss over a bit of black pudding with apple sauce !'. Apple sauce, or stewed apple, is another very popular item on the menu in Brussels, though it is usually eaten at home, again with a pork chop or sausages, and preferably chips.

Volumes could be written on the subject of chips —and indeed, they already have been. But amongst all the theories, one thing is clear: Brussels is the capital of the country where the best chips in the world are made ! In all corners of the globe, people fall for our crispy twice-fried chips. Yet another delicious dish that weight-watchers should avoid ! They still talk about

it in Tokyo, where Belgium presented her chips at the World Exhibition. The elegantly slim hostesses selling them were all ten to twenty kilos heavier by the end of the exhibition...

Chips and mussels are a marriage made in heaven. And of course, 'Mussels means Brussels'.

The most famous restaurants in Brussels are not necessarily the best address for mussels. For us, and for many others in Brussels too, THE place for mussels is 'Chez Henri' in the Vlaamse Steenweg 113: completely unknown to non-locals. Then there is of course 'Chez Léon' in the Beenhouwerstraat, which claims to be the Mecca of mussels-with-chips for day trippers and tourists. But the people of Mecca will not have to come all the way to Brussels for much longer, since 'Chez Léon' is opening mussel

restaurants all over the world, from Moscow to the Champs Elysées, and from New York to Tokyo.

Some Brussels mussel restaurants serve these versatile little creatures in dozens of different ways. For connoisseurs with a taste for 'moules parquées', raw from the shell, one place to find them is at a stall parked in the tiny Katelijneplein, usually near the Vismarkt or Fish Market.

This delicious morsel, to be eaten standing and straight from the shell, can also be found by the many 'caracolemadammen' ('snail ladies'), who in fact sell 'escargots' and a variety of cockles and mussels and winkles and shellfish of all kinds. Together with your mussels, you will be handed a couple of pins. They are not to stick in your hat, but to extract the tender mouthful from its shell. Between mussels, savour a sip of the aromatic celery stock flavoured with a selection of herbs which is one of the best-kept family secrets in Brussels. Customer relations, you might say, or how the 'caracolemadammen' keep their clients faithful for life... Many regular customers turn up every day for their daily portion, bringing the 'caracolemadam' up to date with the latest instalment of their life story: table talk on the street corner.

'Boestring' smells fishy too, and it is in fact simply smoked herring with a little of this and that. In days gone by, it was the food of the poor, like so many other local dishes. Today it can be enjoyed as a gourmet dish in many of the fish restaurants on the Vismarkt.

'Bustling Brussels'... but no sign of 'Brusselians'.
Tourist 'chefs' flourish their ladles in Beenhouwersstraat (Butchers' Street)
and the surrounding area.

The Korte Beenhouwersstraat (Short Butchers' Street) is charming and
subdued and lined with restaurants. This little street looks attractive,
though more of another era and one wouldn't suspect it was Brussels.

57

Another dish frequently on the menu is 'asperges à la flamande' —asparagus in the Flemish manner. Although this is not a speciality of Brussels alone, Brussels was originally a Flemish town, which justifies its inclusion here.

Chicory or witloof —famous as far afield as the better restaurants of New York— is cultivated a stone's throw from Brussels. It is eaten raw as a salad, accompanied by chips (of course), or braised with a lump of sugar from neighbouring Tienen.

There is certainly no shortage of restaurants in Europe's capital. Brussels probably has the highest concentration of restaurants in the world, and at the very least it is the city with the widest variety of different cuisines, from the local to the highly exotic. It is hard to think of a nation or ethnic minority that does not have something bubbling on the stove or steaming in the kitchen of a restaurant somewhere in the capital.

Gastronomes converge on the Sunday market in South Brussels from far and wide. There are more olives sold there than in Italy, and the stalls heaped with herbs and spices perfume the air with a tantalising blend of aromas from Africa, Asia Minor and the Far East. The creatures which can be seen in the Zoo in Antwerp, can probably also be eaten in some restaurant somewhere in Brussels: antelope, new-born monkeys, snake, giraffe... And if you fancy a meal of flowers, don't eat the flower arrangements but try one of the restaurants where flowers are on the menu. It may sound like a pastime for the idle rich, but it is said to be delicious !

Brussels really does have something for everyone. But for those who have lost their heart to the true Burgundian cuisine of Brussels, it can be enjoyed at a modest price in restaurants like 'Chez Jean' in the Hoedenmakersstraat near the Grote Markt. Try it and you will see what I mean: a comfortable, homely interior without any showy pomp and circumstance, but attractively laid tables and a satisfying, old-fashioned Burgundian meal in the traditional middle class Brussels style. On an ordinary weekday, you may find yourself dispatching a good piece of meat cheek by jowl with the mayor of Brussels and opposite a Royal jeweller.

But if you want pomp and circumstance, you can have it. 'De Zwaan' on the Grote Markt, for instance, where Victor Hugo and Karl Marx once hung out, and where the Belgian Workers' Party was founded. And then of course there are the elegant delights of the unequalled 'Comme chez Soi' on the Rouppéplein. Its Art Nouveau decor is a feast for the eye, and the celebrated 'mousses' of master-chef Pierre Wynants are said to be famous the world over. Heads of state have been known to have him flown over, complete with pots and pans and assistant potato-peelers, to cook for them in their own kitchen: after all, it's cheaper to eat at home, isn't it ?

And for those who won't or can't pay so much, there are always the chip shops —try them ! They're good !

THE BURGUNDY OF BEER

Although no wine is made in Brussels, substantial quantities of wine are drunk in the restaurants of the capital.

Tsar Peter the Great would bear me out in this. Long, long ago, he was on his way home after a night in Brussels where the wine flowed freely, taking a carafe with him 'for the road'. He made it to the park in front of the ducal palace, and collapsed in the fountain, where he was discovered the next morning. Because the noble wine had mingled with the water of the fountain, the Tsar of all Russia later conferred a knighthood on the noble pool.

But meals are often accompanied by beer rather than wine in Brussels. Beer fits every occasion: to chase off a hangover, to drink with a meal, on a pavement café, over lunch. Count them all up, and they amount to quite a few pints —and then you can spend the whole night tasting some of the bewildering assortment of types and brands of beer available in Brussels. And some of these are sure to be local brews.

Although Brussels today is proud to have two beer and brewing museums, there is no longer much to be seen in the way of breweries or large beer cellars in the town. But you can pay a highly informative visit —including beer-tasting— to the *Brewery Museum* on the Grote Markt or the *Brussels Geuze Museum* in the Gheudestraat 56.

Any right-minded visitor to Brussels is bound to succumb to the temptation to taste at least the local brews like geuze, faro, raspberry beer, kriek (cherry beer) and lambiek. Lambiek is brewed from a mixture of wheat, malted barley and hop, and a blend of lambiek at various stages of maturity gives us geuze — 'the burgundy among

The 'Mort Subite', Brussels'
most authentic café near
St. Michael's Cathedral.

Café 'Falstaff'. You just have to
come here to try a lambic, a typical
Brussels beer. Or a 'geuze', a 'faro'
or a 'kriek' (black cherry beer).

The people of Brussels still buy their bread from the 'warm baker's' - even at this modern bakery in the trendy Dansaertstraat.

beers' or 'our champagne'. Faro is lambiek with the addition of candied sugar; it has a young flavour and fruity aroma. At the end of July, cherries from Schaarbeek, one of the nineteen 'principalities' of Brussels, are put to soak in Lambiek for six months until they have completely dissolved. This is what we call 'kriek'. Repeat the same process with raspberries instead of cherries, and you have 'frambozenkriek': raspberry beer.

Within the precincts of Brussels, various holy places are preserved as temples or museums of local beer. No beer pilgrimage would be complete without a visit to 'A la Mort Subite' on the Warmoesberg. Local beer is served here with the unique Brussels cheese, which is popularly known as 'stinkerkeis' or stinking cheese in honour of its powerful olfactory onslaught. This is a cheese which should be savoured at its best, i.e. after decomposition has already set in: which explains a lot. Brown bread with quark ('fromage frais') from just up the road in Brabant is certainly worth tasting too, or a mixture of the two cheeses, served with spring onions and radishes.

Almost all the kings of Belgium have drunk a geuze in this establishment, and the same is true of 'Les Deux Bécasses' in the Taborastraat, where similar specialities are served. Local beers are also tapped in the welcoming old-fashioned atmosphere of the little pubs in the Geschenkengang and Sint-Nikolaasgang shopping galleries.

And when the bread is finished, then in Brussels they eat biscuits. 'Dandoy' is a gem of an institution and by far the most attractive shop of its kind in the capital... in Boterstraat (Butter Street), of course. 'Pains à la Grecque' is not Greek at all, but from the baker on the 'grecht' which in Brussels Flemish means 'canalside'. 'Speculaas' (spiced biscuits) is also a Brussels invention !

Pralines from Brussels are flown across the ocean and even sold singly in other parts of the world... In Brussels they are eaten by the kilo. Wittamer also sells the capital's most delicious pastries.

MY KINGDOM
FOR A CHOCOLATE

In Belgium, the feast of Saint Nicholas (our Santa Claus) immediately conjures up a vision of chocolate. No shortage of that in Brussels ! There is hardly a street where you are safe from the temptation of a chocolate shop, with that irresistible aroma and rich array of 'pralines' or chocolates unequalled anywhere in the world. Across the ocean, these chocolate delights are so highly prized as a luxury item that they are even sold singly ! 'Godiva' chocolates are accorded the same hushed awe as the most prestigious wine appellations, champagne and caviar. It is worth making a detour to visit 'Neuhaus', the nineteenth century chocolate shop in the Koninginnegalerij —go on, spoil yourself ! Or for a wide assortment of white chocolates, *the* address is 'Corné Toison d'Or'. 'Mary' in the Koningstraat supplies chocolates to the royal palace, while 'Leonidas' chocolates are consumed by the kilo at all levels of Belgian society, and also through up-market outlets in the most elegant stores elsewhere in Europe. Even the ordinary bars of 'Côte d'Or' chocolate with their famous elephant trademark are enough to make many of us forget the calorie count and our livers.

Ice cream has never been a ruling passion in Brussels, but we have been known to melt for a really good cake... test your resistance at 'Wittamer' on the Zavel.

And where could one find a better address for biscuits than in the Boterstraat (Butter Street) ? The biscuit shop 'De Paerle' dates from 1696, and the Dandoy family has been baking the best biscuits in Brussels there since 1858. Their 'pain à la grecque' is famous; the name has nothing to do with Greece, but refers to the 'grecht', which is Brussels dialect for 'gracht' or canal. Stand in front of their shop window and admire the magnificent creations in 'speculaas', a spicy type of biscuit from which very decorative 'gingerbread men' are made, and many other designs. Speculaas is said to have been invented in Brussels, in the Bergstraat, where baker Van den Spiegel plied his trade. His name is 'de speculo' in Latin, which is claimed to be root of 'speculaas'.

Brussels is in a class of its own in the world when it comes to eating and drinking and gastronomic indulgence: in this respect, Brussels is worth more than one mass !

Apparently there is as much of 'God' as there is of 'diva' in a 'Godiva' praline.

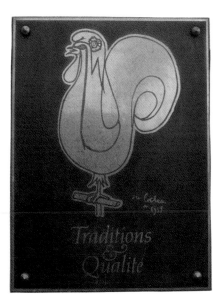

The signboard at the entrance to top restaurant 'Comme chez Soi' on the Rouppeplein. A drawing by Cocteau.

'Comme chez Soi' with its chef Pierre Wynants is one of Belgium's and the world's best restaurants and you need to book weeks in advance.

Horses and carriages riding over the cobblestones of the Grote Markt (main square) complete the picture of bygone days.

The most beautiful market square on earth.
There is no doubt about it, particularly when decked with its annual carpet of begonias from the city of Ghent.

The most beautiful market square in the world

The market square has always played an important role in the history of European towns, particularly when it is located in the centre of town, like the Grote Markt in Brussels.

The Grote Markt started life as a sandbank between two little rivers, where the 'Niedermerct' was set up in the tenth century on drained marshland. In the eleventh century, this market still lay outside the defensive wall built around the 'Sint-Goriks Castrum' or fortified camp which was the cradle of Brussels. Two important trading routes ran through Brussels: one between France and the Rhinelands and the other between Brabant and Holland.

The square did not always have the regular layout it has today; it was not until the fourteenth century that some order began to emerge. Before that, it was simply a cluster of wooden houses with gardens around: quite countrified, according to modern standards.

The Grote Markt in Brussels still plays an important role in public life. Heads of State and the great and the good of this world come and look out over this beautiful square from the balcony of the Town Hall. Princes, dukes, governors, kings, emperors, popes and sporting heroes are all welcomed and honoured here. Victor Hugo once lived in one of the houses on this square, and the Belgian Workers' Party was founded in another, where Karl Marx gave readings from 'Das Kapital'. But the Grote Markt has another side to its character too: it has also been the scene of historical executions and vandalistic 'battles'.

It can be seen in all its glory when the annual sixteenth century 'Ommegang' or pageant slowly winds over the cobblestones, or in December, when a real Kempen farmhouse is erected for the Christmas crib. Then the atmosphere in the square breathes a magnificent solemnity.

But the Grote Markt is at its best every day of the week (except Monday), when it is filled with the brilliant colours of the flower stalls under their red-and-green parasols —the colours of the city.

Without a shadow of doubt, the most beautiful square on earth is the Grote Markt in the heart of Brussels ! An absolute must for the tourist, together with Manneken Pis and Atomium. The people of Brussels themselves always refer to 'the most beautiful square in the world', and who would argue with them ? The elegant façades around the square have an impressive charm that still reflects the power and wealth of the ancient guilds.

Guides may often tell their flock of tourists that the guild houses around the Grote Markt date from the Middle Ages, but with the exception of the Gothic Town Hall, all the buildings on the square in fact date from the end of the seventeenth century. In 1695 the town was bombarded by Field Marshal De Villeroy on the orders of the French 'sun king' Louis XIV. No less than 60,000 troops bombarded the heart of Brussels for two whole days, reducing thousands of houses to ashes and leaving little intact on the Grote Markt.

But not for long: in less than five years, the burghers and guilds had rebuilt their market square from

left
The French Sun King, Louis XIV, had city and market razed to the ground in an act of vengeance in 1695. Even before the turn of the century in 1770, the brilliance and splendour of Brussels Grote Markt (main square) shone more brightly than the sun. Even the vengeful French King did not have a square like this. Yet the rebuilding of the guild houses heralded the end of the power of the guilds and age-old trades !

below
No gold was spared to restore the ancient dazzle and brilliance to this façade which once belonged to the extremely powerful Dukes of Brabant. More than 40,000 little leaves of this precious metal were stuck on and polished with the patience of saints and a great deal of skill.

the ashes, even more glorious than before. Brussels made a triumphant entry into the Age of Enlightenment with a central square which was to remain unrivalled throughout the world. Today, every inhabitant of Brussels is convinced that no other city could ever succeed in building such a varied and yet harmonious architectural creation as their own Grote Markt.

But after the completion of the Grote Markt with the proud guildhalls risen again in even more magnificence than before, the power and the glory of the guilds began to wane once and for all. And it is no less than a wonder that the old façades have survived at all, since so many of the owners of premises on the Grote Markt were bitten with the urge to modernise their property to celebrate Belgian Independence.

A TOUR OF
THE GROTE MARKT

The Town Hall of Brussels is one of the most beautiful examples of Gothic architecture in Europe. The first stone was laid on 4 March 1444 and the last in 1451. The architect is unknown, but the creator of the spire of the Town Hall was Jan Van Ruysbroeck. It took from 1449 to 1455 to complete the magnificent stone tracery. High up on top, the wind vane in the form of St Michael killing the dragon can still be seen.

Guildhalls. Clockwise, starting from the Town Hall: De Vos (fox), De Hoorn (horn), De Wolvin (she-wolf), De Zak (bag), De Kruiwagen (wheelbarrow), Den

The spontaneous artistic expression in the streets and squares of Brussels is wonderful, even if it is 'art' with a small 'a'.

Coninck van Spagnien (king of Spain), Den Ezel (donkey), Sinte-Barbara (Saint Barbara), Den Eyck (oak tree), De Kleine Vos (little fox), De Pauw (peacock), Den Helm (helmet), Het Broodhuis (bread hall), De Kroon (crown), De Duif (dove), Het Cleermaekershuis (tailors' hall), Den Engel (angel), Jozef en Anna (Joseph and Anna), Den Hert (hart) and De Wage (weighhouse). Then there is the large complex of the House of the Dukes of Brabant, including De Borse (purse), De Heuvel (hill), De Tinnen Pot (pewter pot), De Windmolen (windmill), De Fortuyne (Fortune), De Cluyse (hermitage) and De Faem (fame). Next to that there is De Koning van Beieren (king of Bavaria), De Bergh Thabor (Mount Tabor), De Roos (rose), De Gulden Boom (golden tree), De Zwaan (swan) and De Ster (star).

THE GROTE MARKT AND THE MAGICAL NUMBER 7

Seven streets lead onto the Grote Markt, and it is even claimed that there were once seven secret entrance gates. Seven different markets were held here in succession over the ages. Seven guildhalls bear the name of an animal. Seven aldermen ruled from the Town Hall in the Middle Ages, and their records were kept in the 'boec metden seven slote' —the book with the seven locks. Every Friday, seven musicians played in the Town Hall, and on the façade of the 'King of Spain' seven allegorical statues can be seen. When there was still a fountain on the Grote Markt, it was one of the seven squares in Brussels where water played.

The Brussels Exchange was originally built to display the confidence of the new bourgeoisie and the energetic approach of the young state of Belgium. Rodin was one of the sculptors responsible for the frescoes and groups of figures.

Following pages
Tourists rob the Grote Markt (main square) of its majesty and history with their eyes and cameras.
Every day the people of Brussels pass on titbits of information to visitors about their city, as if the centuries had changed nothing.

The Royal Academy fosters 'Culture with a capital C'. In contrast to this uninhibited young man in her garden, the 'old lady' of the 'Fine Arts, Letters and Sciences' does not lay herself bare so easily.

Culture with or without a capital 'C'

Walking around in the centre of Brussels, one can immediately see that it has a rich cultural past. The palace of the Dukes of Burgundy on the Coudenberg was once the richest court in Europe, and perhaps even the world. The artists of the age had created a palace of unheard-of luxury and comfort, bulging with the riches of a magnificent art collection.

In fact, Brussels was never short of rulers, princes and oppressors who had the means to keep the artistic community hard at work. The burghers themselves, and their municipal authorities also commissioned a host of works of art from the foremost artists of the time —artists whose works now adorn the walls of the great international museums and art collections.

Pieter Breughel the Elder and a whole dynasty of painters after him, including the Teniers clan (related by marriage) and the unsurpassed Rogier Van der Weyden, now hang from the most expensive picture rails in the world. They all lived and worked in Brussels —and there were so many more of them !

Like many other great cities, Brussels too has a two-speed cultural life. There is culture with a capital 'C' and culture with a small 'c', and these two circuits operate peacefully side by side, as if it had always been that way.

THE OPERA... THE OPERA !

In recent years, the cultural flagship has been the Brussels opera house, popularly known as the 'Munt' (= Mint) or 'Muntschouwburg' because it stands on the site of the old mint in the Muntplein, where the coins of the realm —and those of the current foreign ruler— were minted.

In 1830, this opera house was the scene of the starting signal which unleashed the Belgian revolution. Malicious tongues would have it that the opera 'De Stomme van Portici' was such an abysmal production and the singers so off-key that the Brussels audience stormed out in disgust, put a light to the fuse and threw the Spanish oppressor out in an violent fit of its famous 'Spanish pique' ! So the nation owes its independence to an operatic flop... true or false, it makes a good story.

Since then, the fortunes of the Brussels opera has had many ups and downs. In recent years, it has enjoyed a meteoric rise to success, and is presently regarded as one of the leading opera houses in the world. Whole train-loads of opera buffs roll in even from Paris to pay homage to its supremacy !

above
Culture is sometimes like an open, glass house, like this splendid orangery and the park attached to the Herb Garden.

right
It is impossible to imagine Brussels any more without the raging popularity of football. Behind the façade of this tribunal is Heizel Stadium, famous for its legendary matches and infamous for its tragic Heizel drama.

Over the centuries and throughout the world, Belgian artists have built up a good reputation for themselves.

The sounds of this bard's cabaret song ring out between the antique and the weekly Zavel (Sablon) market. Even dogs with practised ears stop short.

Besides being Brussels' most handsome weather vane, with powerful wing-beat the gold 'Genius of the Fine Arts' also plays guardian angel to the treasures of the Museum of Ancient Art.

Brussels has hundreds of museums. Many of these 'custodial houses' lead a hidden existence. Behind this façade with its modest signboard, the Museum of Costumes and Lace houses a splendid collection of clothes and lacework.

OUR HERITAGE ON ICE

Brussels is studded with great museum collections, where our cultural heritage is put on ice for future generations. These rich collections are spread over more than a hundred large museums, plus a host of smaller ones, which are no less fascinating than their big brothers. To visit them all in a year, you would have to visit an average of three museums a week the whole year long! The exhibits are extremely wide-ranging, and many museums are regarded as leading establishments in their field.

The *Bibliotheca Wittockiana* is a good example of this: a superb collection housed in a superb piece of architecture. A shrine which attracts bibliophiles from all corners of the world.

Another museum which deserves special mention is the *David and Alice Van Buuren Museum*, an Art Deco dream: a private residence blending classical masterpieces with the modern style of architecture of the interbellum period, set in a series of eight different gardens. The *Museum of the Heart - Boyadjian* is a bijou collection focusing on the heart, and the happy atmosphere of the elegantly housed *Strip Cartoon museum* will appeal to the child in us all. For those who want to delve into the history of Brussels, the second floor of the Municipal Museum in the *Broodhuis* a real treasure-trove.

Naturally, the prestigious collections in the *Museum of Ancient Art* exert a powerful attraction, with works by Breughel, Rubens, Van Dyck and Teniers, as well as the masterpieces of unfaltering precision bequeathed to us by the Flemish Primitives. The turn-of-the-century school of art will pull in many art-lovers —and who could resist the primitive power of so many of the Flemish Expressionists ?

The former department store, Waucques, designed by Victor Horta, is now the home of the world's first and only comic strip museum.

Belgium is the capital city of the ninth art, the comic strip story.
And, of course, the Comic Strip Museum would not be complete without the Kuifje moon rocket,
drawn by Hergé.

THE LONGEST FAIR

If we can believe the scenes depicted on Breughel's canvases, there was always something to celebrate in the capital of Brabant in the good old days. There were a thousand and one excuses for organising a party with food and free drinks all round, and much letting-down of hair and dancing in the eat-drink-and-be-merry tradition. There was even a period in the history of the city when there were almost more feast days than working days. However, when Austrian sovereigns (among others) imposed their rule, they soon put a stop to all that by forcing these spontaneous outbursts into a straitjacket of stern regulation.

Nevertheless, there is still no shortage of fairs and local festivals in Brussels. The biggest of them all is the six-week *Kermis van het Zuid*: the south Brussels funfair, or annual fair. The extravagant and costly funfair machinery erected there has to be seen to be believed: more than two kilometres of it, from modest stalls to vast, grotesque creations. No wonder they call it the longest funfair in the world !

THE BIGGEST BOOK FAIR AND THE BIGGEST CINEMA

The annual *International Book Fair of Brussels* is the largest book fair in the world with access for the general public. Even if the purely professional trade fair in Frankfurt is included, the Brussels fair is still number two in the world stakes. It is also the fair with the most exhibits from the Latin world. This grandiose book festival is held in March every year.

Brussels may not be Hollywood, but it has the largest cinema complex in the world. At 'Kineapolis' on the Heizel, no fewer than 26 films are showing at the same time. So many to choose from ! Kineapolis was an instant success, but this siphoned off the lifeblood of the downtown cinemas, who followed the sad example of the theatres in the town centre and gently expired. This was a great pity, because their demise deprived the town centre of a large part of its cultural life.

DE OMMEGANG OR PAGEANT

If a procession parades through the streets of Brussels nowadays, it usually has less to do with folklore than with the time-honoured custom of taking to the streets as soon as things get difficult, or when discontent raises its ugly head. But although the people of Brussels enjoy a good grumble now and then, they do not only take to the streets for demonstrations. They also come out in force to portray the glorious history of their city, and to remind fellow-citizens, travellers and tourists that Brussels is a proud city with a thousand years of history behind it. The fame and glory of past ages are evoked in the annual *Ommegang* or pageant which winds through the streets of Brussels at the beginning of July, whatever the weather, to reach a climax on the Grote Markt. There the pageant is welcomed from on high by real live noblemen and other prominent burghers of Brussels up in their VIP grandstand. Because the historical pageant is a great box office success, it is held twice in the same week.

Brussels has no film studios, but it does have the largest cinema complex in the whole world.

The custom dates back to 1348, when the miraculous statue of 'Our Dear Lady on the Stick' arrived in Brussels by boat and was installed in the Zavel church. One Beatrijs Soetkens had kidnapped the statue in Antwerp, on the orders of persons unknown. To the people of Antwerp, who had to manage from then onwards without the miraculous powers of their Dear Lady, the people of Brussels

promised with much honest heart-crossing that every year they would honour the statue by carrying her through the streets of the city. And so they did, and still do today.

Exhibits in the Natural Science Museum in the Vautierstraat include a unique collection of iguanodons.

On show in the World Palace of the Automobile, Autoworld for short, are the finest German, Italian, French and, above all, American cars.

right
The greenhouses in the Herb Garden in Koningstraat (King's Street) were built in 1826.

The daily Flea Market on the Vossenplein (Fox Square), in the midst of the working-class Marollen district, is currently very much in vogue. The weekend markets should not be missed.

right
Toone Theatre is just a puppet theatre.
In a dark little room at the end of this typical Brussels 'passageway', real 'Brusselians' pull the strings.

MARIONETTES

For centuries, foreign masters pulled the strings and called the tune in Brussels. But the people of Brussels obviously wanted a turn at the strings too, and designed marionettes who would dance to *their* tune for a change ! Perhaps that is how the puppet theatres of Brussels came into being...

At one time, the genre was in decline and almost forgotten. But a couple of typically Brussels puppeteers refused to give up, and

decided to try to save the fine art of marionette puppetry for posterity. They were successful, and that is how it came about that Brussels now has two famous marionette theatres where the puppets speak other languages as well as Brussels dialect ! They also perform in German and English and even in modern 'Franglais'.

Theater Toone is now in the seventh generation, and Theater Perruchet has its own academy of puppetry and *International Marionette Museum*. At the

beginning of 1991, a new 'poesjenelle' or marionette theatre was opened opposite Manneken Pis. The genre is obviously growing in popularity, and seeking international recognition far afield.

'The Passion of Our Lord' and 'Genoveva van Brabant' have been unstoppable box office hits for years. And when the piano accompaniment is played by the piano virtuoso Pierre Volondat, theatre-with-strings really breaks into the international class !

Paintings are the main treasures housed behind the classical façade of the Museum of Ancient Art in Regentschapsstraat (Regency Street), where Rubens is given a place of honour.

The Museum of Modern Art's stunning collection of modern paintings is displayed in a well with glass walls and penetrates six floors deep into the ground.

Both Belgian and foreign painters are well represented at the Museum of Modern Art.

Over the last few years, the people of Brussels have developed a curious habit of stowing away their artistic and cultural heritage underground. Of course, a great deal is stored in museum cellars and underground art reserves, because there is far too much to display all at once. But what I am talking about are the exhibits, not the reserves: more and more of our cultural heritage seems to be on show underground these days. Underground museums are booming!

There is the *Museum of Modern Art*, six cellars deep under the Museumplein. Under the cobblestones of the Koningsplein, where the entrance to this museum can be found, a new museum will soon be taking shape, and on the other side of the same square, work is already underway on a new religious museum under the church of Sint-Jacob-op-de-Coudenberg.

A vast underground *Museum of Science and Technology* is planned for the Heizel, and the beautifully designed *Sewers Museum* is appropriately located under the Kleine Ring or inner ring road round Brussels.

Despite vociferous opposition, a *Museum of Antiquities* is being built under the pavements in the heart of the city. The *Brewery Museum* has already gone underground in the cellars of the Brouwershuis on the Grote Markt.

The Brussels *Metro* plays a very special role as Belgium's largest underground *Museum of Contemporary Belgian Art*, perhaps also the largest in the world. Dozens of stations are decorated with monumental works by contemporary Belgian artists,

some of whom have works hanging in the most famous and prestigious museums of modern art all over the world. A visit to *Art in the Metro* is warmly recommended —but it can take two days to get round it all !

Then there is the *Museum of Funerary Archaeology*, which is not actually underground, but has certainly buried itself in the cities of the dead to study the particulars of this very special subject. Just as the cities of the living, burial places and churchyards can be a garden of delight for those with a weakness for digging up the history of art and unearthing archaeological finds. Philologists with a taste for tombstone inscriptions can savour the literary aspects of the exhibits, and sociologists can study the social strata of ages past.

In the graveyard in Laken in Brussels, a faithful replica of Rodin's 'Thinker' has been sitting on a tombstone sunk in thought for years. I wonder what he thinks of it all, above ground and below !

left
Two brand-new museums have also been excavated and constructed under Koningsplein (King's Square)
and Sint-Jacob-op-de-Coudenberg (St.James-on-Couden-mountain).
The Museum for Religious Art will be under the church. Access will be made to the excavations,
the remains of a palatial room and the chapel of Emperor Charles,
under the square from a part of the Isabellasstraat.

above
You can ride through this art and culture house: the Brussels metro, the longest underground museum
in the world. Art in the Metro is to be seen in scores of stations, constituting an extensive
Museum for Contemporary Belgian Art. Here we have Stokkel metro station with strip cartoon heroes
from Hergé's Kuifje stories, a cultural export that has no equal.

above left
Brussels' many cities of the dead
are the 'underground' work area
for the Museum for Funeral
Archaeology.

below left
The metropolitan gallery world is
thriving because art is much in
demand in the better sitting rooms
of prosperous 'Brusselians' and
other European residents.

above
The city is a vast open-air museum,
as the Gothic refinement on
Brussels Town Hall exemplifies.

The modern-day pond on Fish Market, with St. Katelijne Church behind it.

Below the 'Finance Tower' of the tax authorities, modern wall art inspires quiet city meditation.

above
Even a quick glance at the Town Hall will confirm that the heart of Brussels is an architectural gem.

right
The picture even just outside the centre is sometimes very different. But this is Brussels the capital city, too.

Without a shadow of doubt, the heart of Brussels with its Grote Markt is an architectural jewel. But sadly, the same cannot be said for the rest of the city. Tourists, travellers and visitors are not far wrong when they observe that if you stray too far from the Grote Markt, you go from the architecturally sublime to the ridiculous.

Brussels was once a beautiful city, the capital of what some call 'the ugliest country in Europe' —an exaggeration, surely. A popular joke has it that Brussels has suffered more devastation since 1945 than during the whole of the second World War. At the beginning of 1991, a demolition squad reduced the oldest house in Brussels, dating from the sixteenth century, to a heap of historic rubble.

There is still architecture from the interbellum period to be enjoyed, and some fifties architecture too, but apart from that, modern architecture and town planning have generally been bad news for Brussels.

Nevertheless, the Brussels Region has cherished a few architectural jewels and miraculous achievements which are the envy of the world. Little original Gothic architecture remains today, except the impressive Town Hall with its slender spire, the glorious Sint-Michiels Cathedral, which really belongs to the popular Sinte-Goedele; Brussels is full of churches. The rest of the architecture in Brussels focuses on façades: mainly frame façades plus a large contingent in the Neoclassical style, interspersed with Neogothic.

But the real architectural wealth of Brussels lies in its many Art Nouveau houses and buildings. Sadly, a great number of them have been demolished, including the world-famous Volkshuis, the magnificent temple of the workers which Victor Horta built for the socialist movement.

Nevertheless, a few of these superb buildings are lovingly preserved as the last fragile remains of an architectural vision which left its stamp on the better streets of Brussels. What this city needs in the context of town planning and architecture is a great urban thinker like Leopold II in his time, and a few really good, renowned architects to come and set the tone in the European capital of the future.

There are a couple of buildings which are particularly worth visiting —perhaps even compulsory visiting ! One of these is the Horta house, where Victor Horta, the famous Art Nouveau architect lived and worked. Then there are the Tassel house and Solvay house, and of course the Stoclet house, which is actually a small palace in the middle of town, built early this century by the great Viennese architect Josef Hoffmann. Both the house and its lady are legendary.

Should you happen to be in Brussels at the end of April or in May, do not miss this opportunity to visit the Koninklijke Serres or royal conservatories. This soaring glass city is one of the most beautiful sights to be seen in Brussels.

Following pages
left
Admirers come to Brussels from all over the world for this little architectural masterpiece. 'Huis Stoclet' (Stoclet House) was built by the famous Viennese architect Josef Hoffmann. The people of Brussels also like to talk about 'Paleis Stoclet' (Stoclet Palace) which is, in fact, nearer the truth.

right
Here art nouveau was fostered by ingenious architects and a rich bourgeoisie which gave them a free hand. Much has been demolished, but nevertheless the people of Brussels and their guests still have some very remarkable gems of superlative architecture.

above
The Royal Palace on Paleizenplein
(Palaces Square), one of Brussels'
loveliest boulevards.

right
Rarely does new architecture in
Brussels lead to reconciliation.

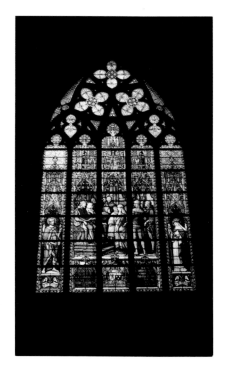

Stained-glass window in
St. Michael's Cathedral.

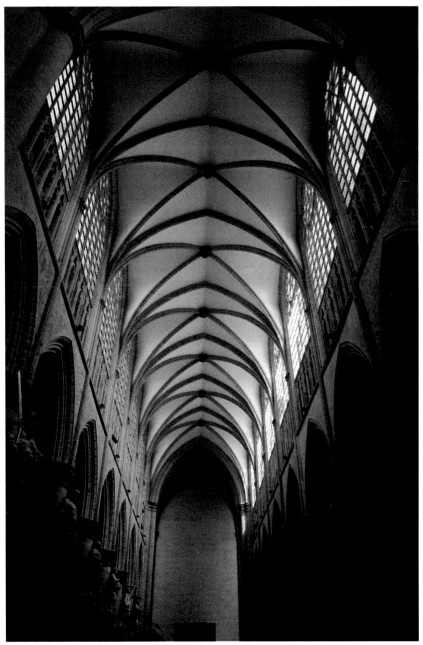

The nave of cathedral,
in early-Gothic style.

left
St. Michael's Cathedral, also called
St. Gudule, is a grandiose
testimony of the historical Gothic.

As Burgomaster of Brussels at the end of the last century,
Karel Buls dedicated a great deal of attention to the architectural patrimony of the capital.
Here we see him sitting by his fountain.

Leopold II gave Belgium a colony; he was also responsible for giving the capital a face. Yet the state could not see its way to footing the bill for this equestrian statue and a collection had to be made.

Previous pages
The Japanese Tower, built by
Leopold II after he visited the
Paris World Fair in 1910.

The Munt Theatre (la Monnaie)
is very much a part of the city's
decor. It was behind these pillars
that the revolution that was to lead
to independence erupted in 1830
after a badly-sung opera !
A few years ago there was more
talk of revolution, but then
with reference to the opera !

The Brussels Palace of Justice was
once the largest edifice in the
world. Below this gigantic building
is the popular Marollen district.

Modest, but charming little alleyways like this one in old Brussels are now few and far between.

above
The gables in Bergstraat (Mountain Street), this ancient trade route, have lost none of their appeal.

right
Martelaarsplein (Martyrs' Square) is an example of eighteenth-century architectural martyrdom.

below
Sharp contrasts in style and urban planning: in the background a modern hospital in Eastern-European style which is in a worse state than the remains of Brussels' first city walls that date back to the thirteenth century.

left
*The St. Hubertus Royal Galleries
served as a model for just about
every large and luxurious shopping
arcade built in Europe at the end of
last century. It is a very happy and
successful mélange of glass, steel,
architecture and perspective.*

right
*In terms of architecture, Brussels is
no longer the pilot city it was in the
nineteenth century. Unfortunately,
architects of international status do
not operate from here any more.
Yet some modern architectural
shapes can be aesthetic, from
certain angles.*

Jubelpark (Jubilee Park).
Concepts about metropolitan architecture had clearly changed by Belgium's fiftieth birthday...

Following pages:
The dome of Koekelberg Basilica
— actually the 'Basilica of the
Sacred Heart' — has become one of
Brussels' landmarks.

left and following pages
Koekelberg Basilica only recently
surrendered its fourth place in the
league table of the world's largest
basilicas.

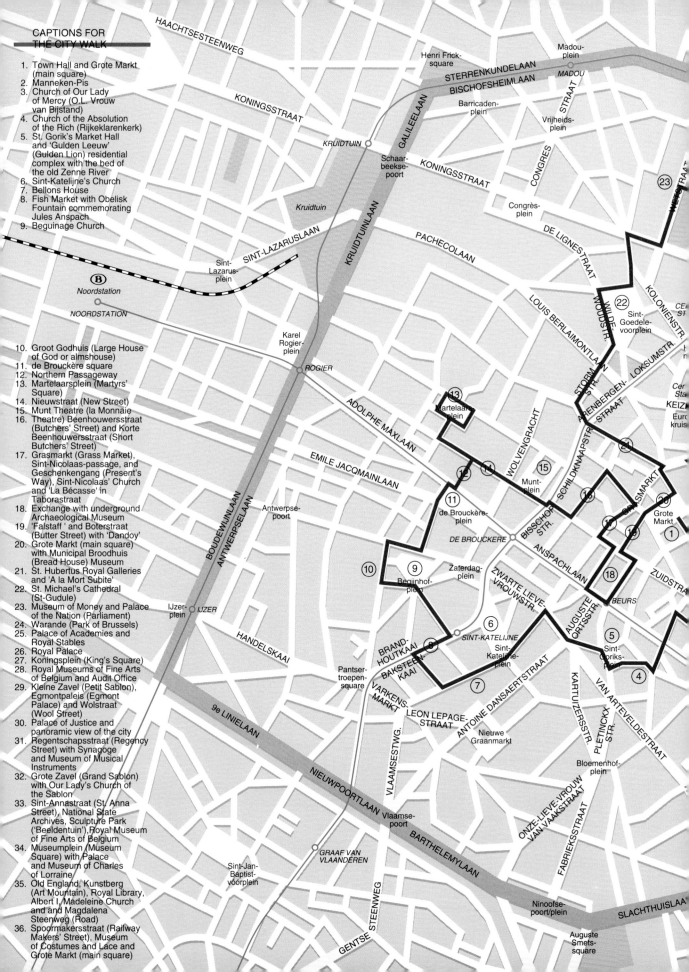

Contents

Info

Tourist Board Brussels
Town Hall
Grote Markt
1000 Brussel
(02) 513 89 40
Administrative department
Eikstraat 10
1000 Brussel
(02) 513 89 40
Fax (02) 514 45 38

Tourist Board Brabant province
Grasmarkt 61
1000 Brussel
(02) 504 04 55

Colophon

This book exists in binded form
or in paperback. Next to the
english edition, a dutch, a french
and a german version are also
published.

Lay-out
Johan Mahieu
Cover
Studio Lannoo
Map
Dirk Billen
Translation
Elizabeth Dijkstra and
Alison Mouthaan

Printed and bound by
Lannoo Tielt - 1993

© Publishers Lannoo, Tielt
Printed in Belgium
D/1993/45/14
ISBN 90 209 1992 X (paperback)
D/1993/45/15
ISBN 90 209 1996 2 (bound)